Prelievo a treni
Libro da colorare

Coloring Pages for Kids

Coloring Pages for Kids
An imprint of Ciparum LLC

Prelievo a treni Libro da colorare
© 2017 Ciparum LLC
All rights reserved.
ISBN-10:1-63589-362-3
ISBN-13:978-1-63589-362-5

Coloring Pages for Kids

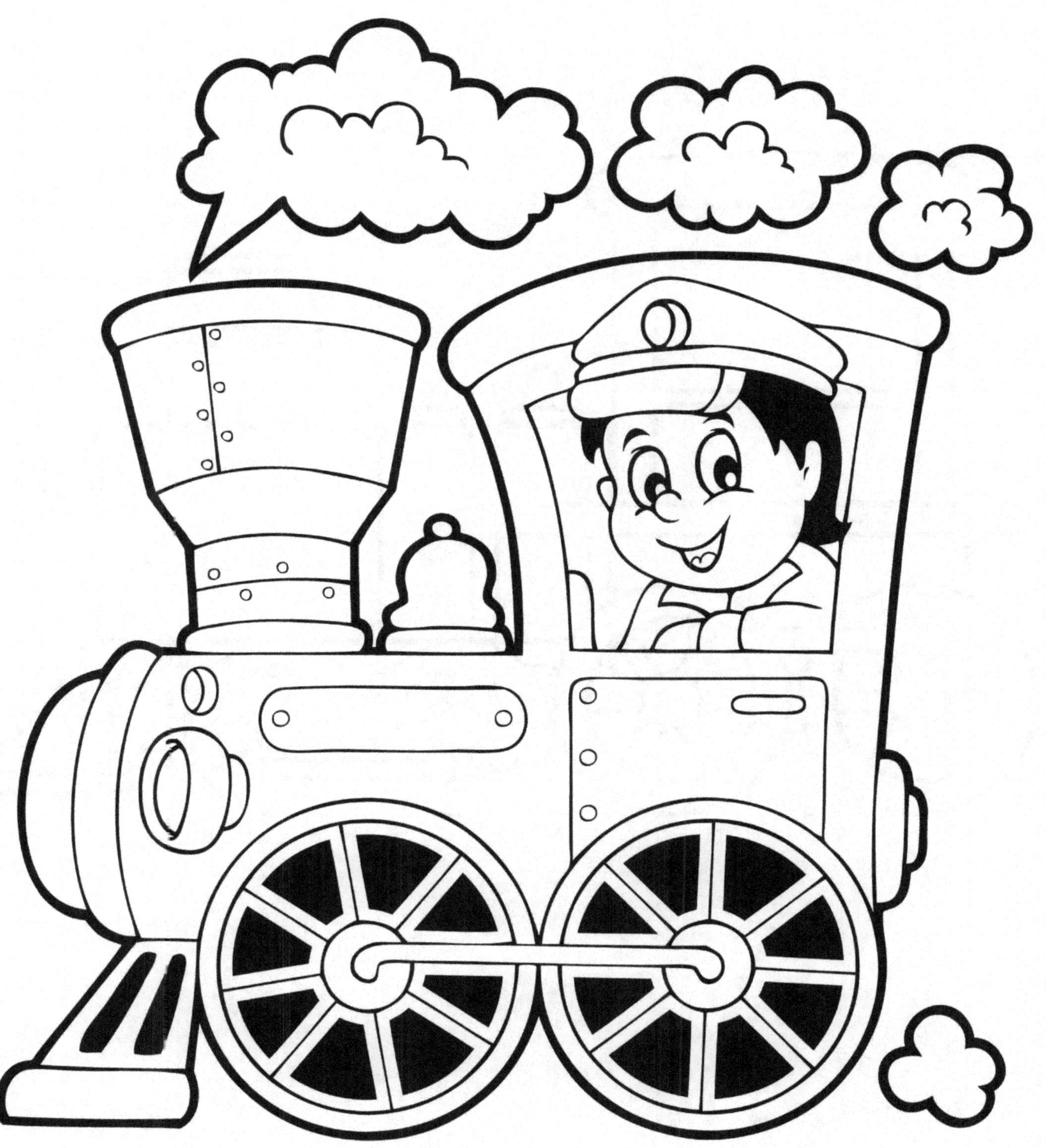

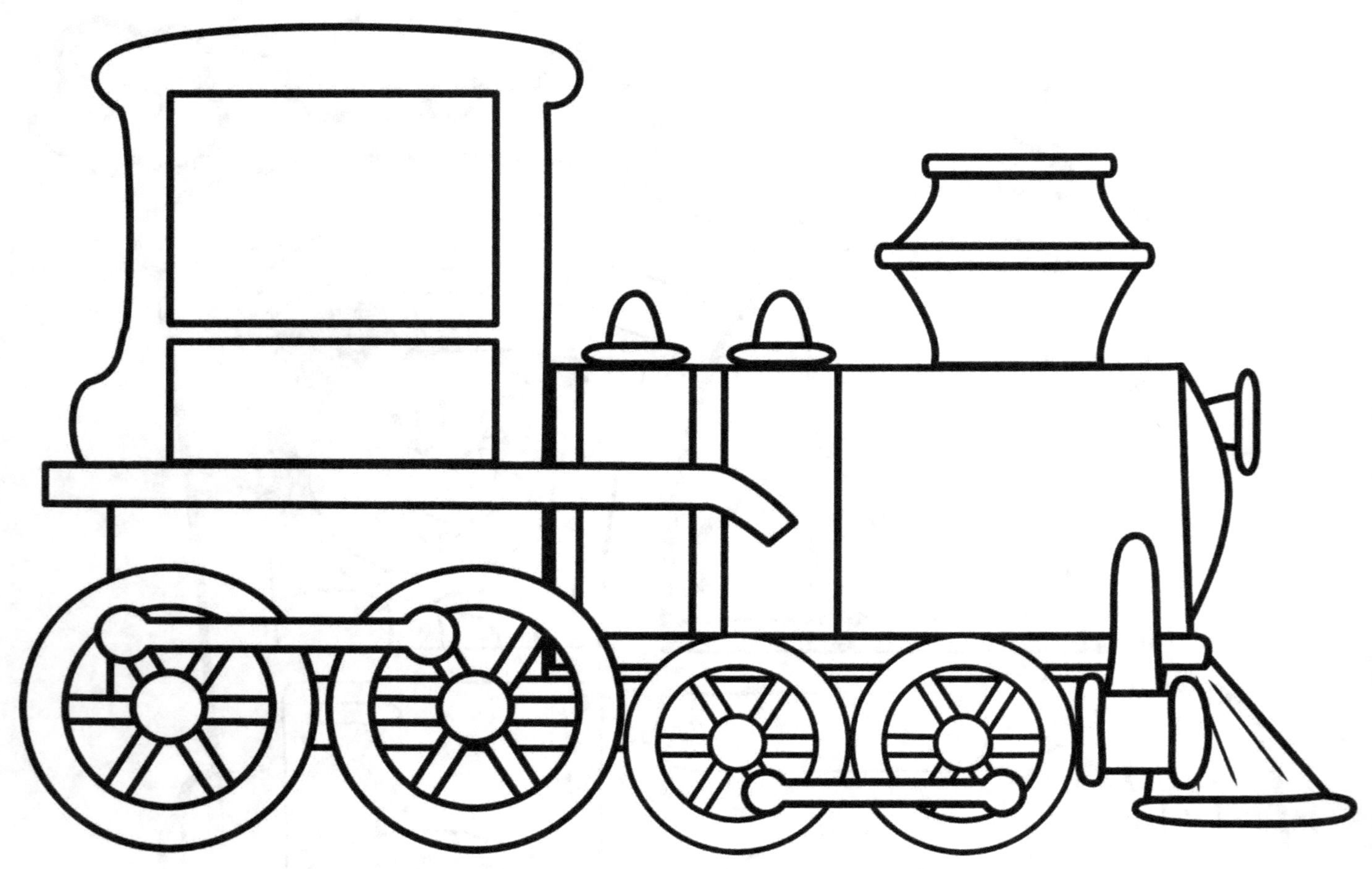

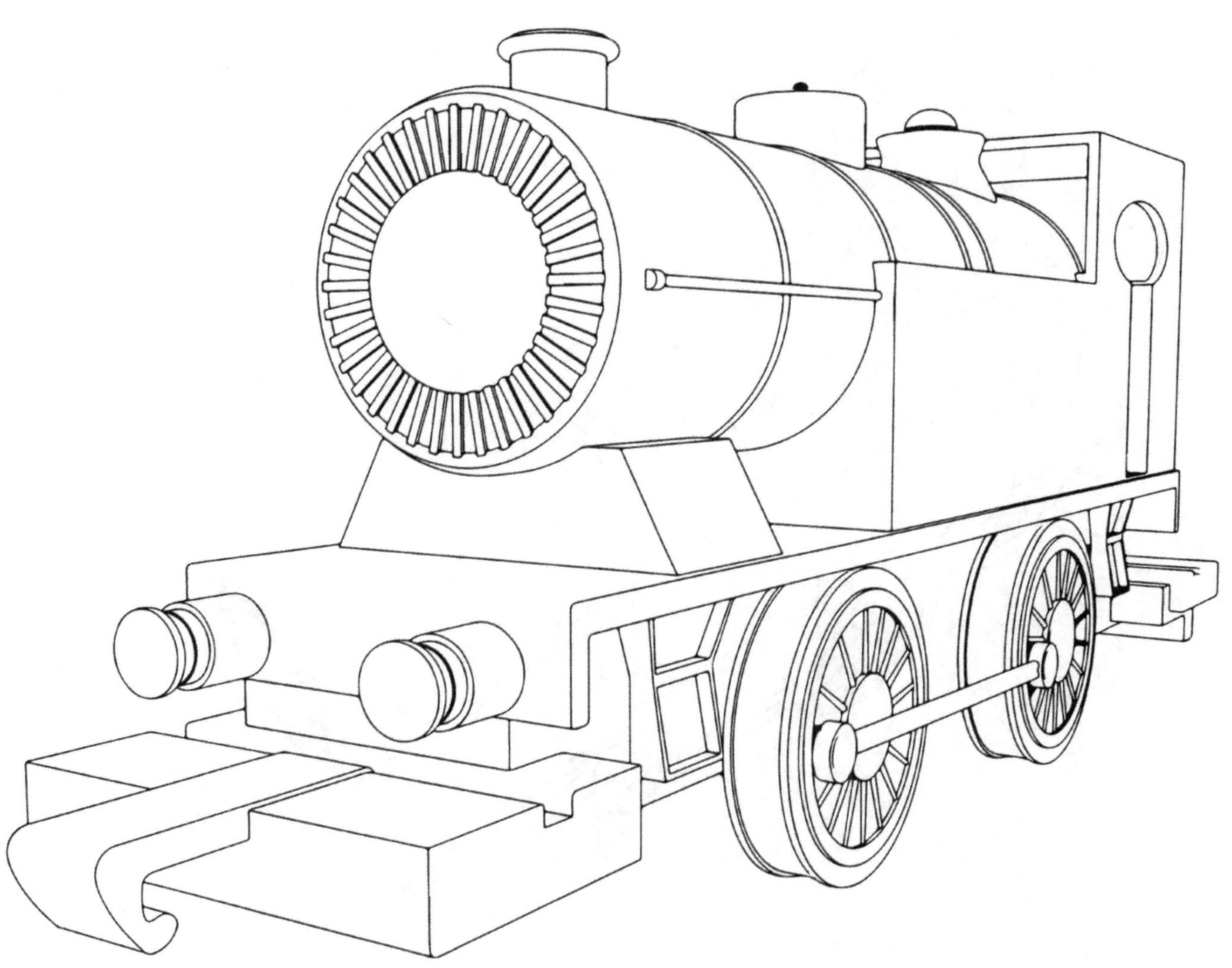

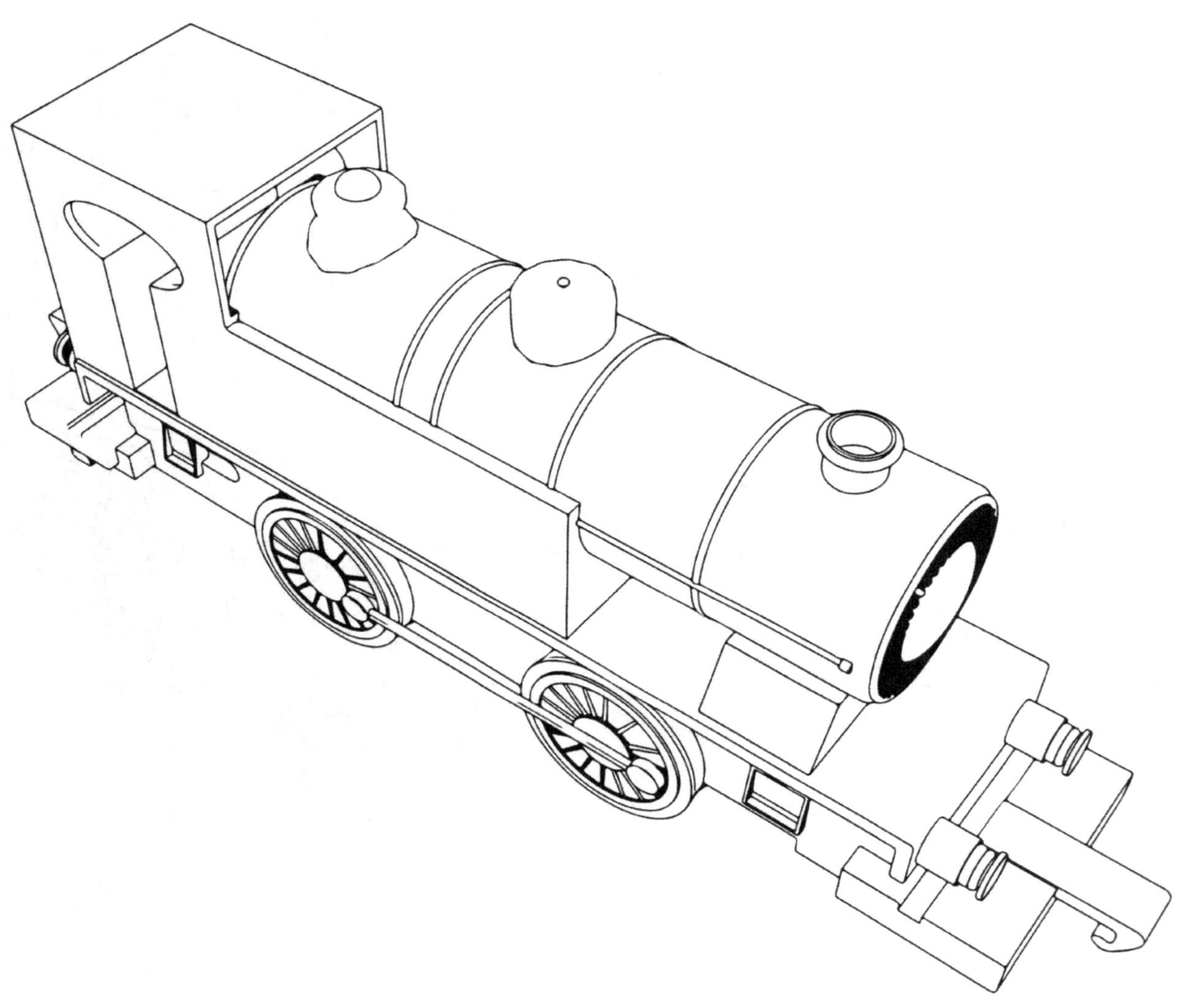

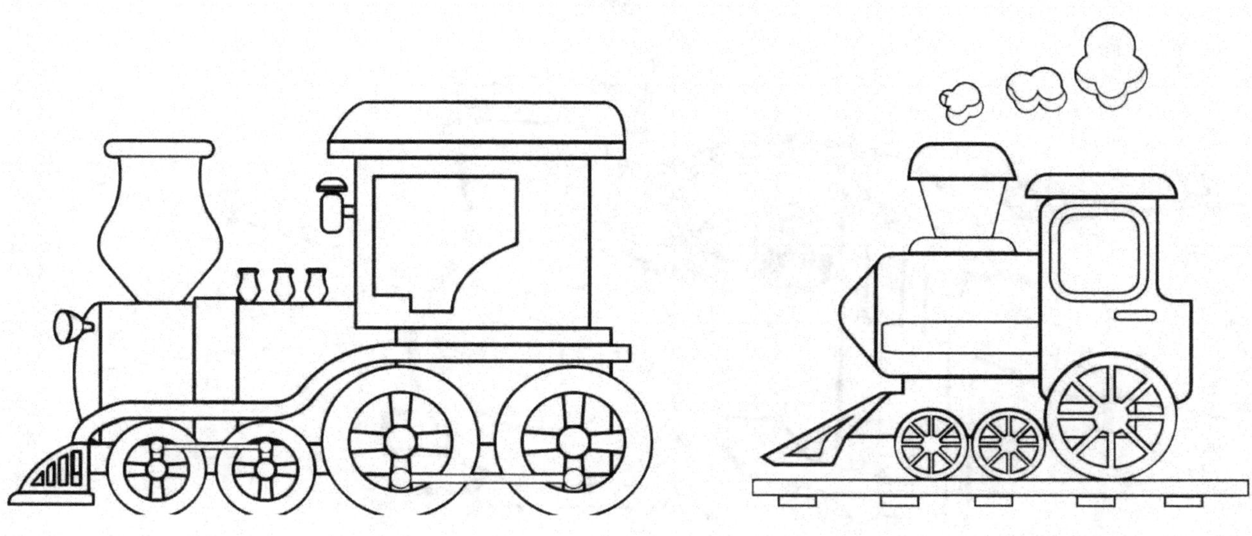

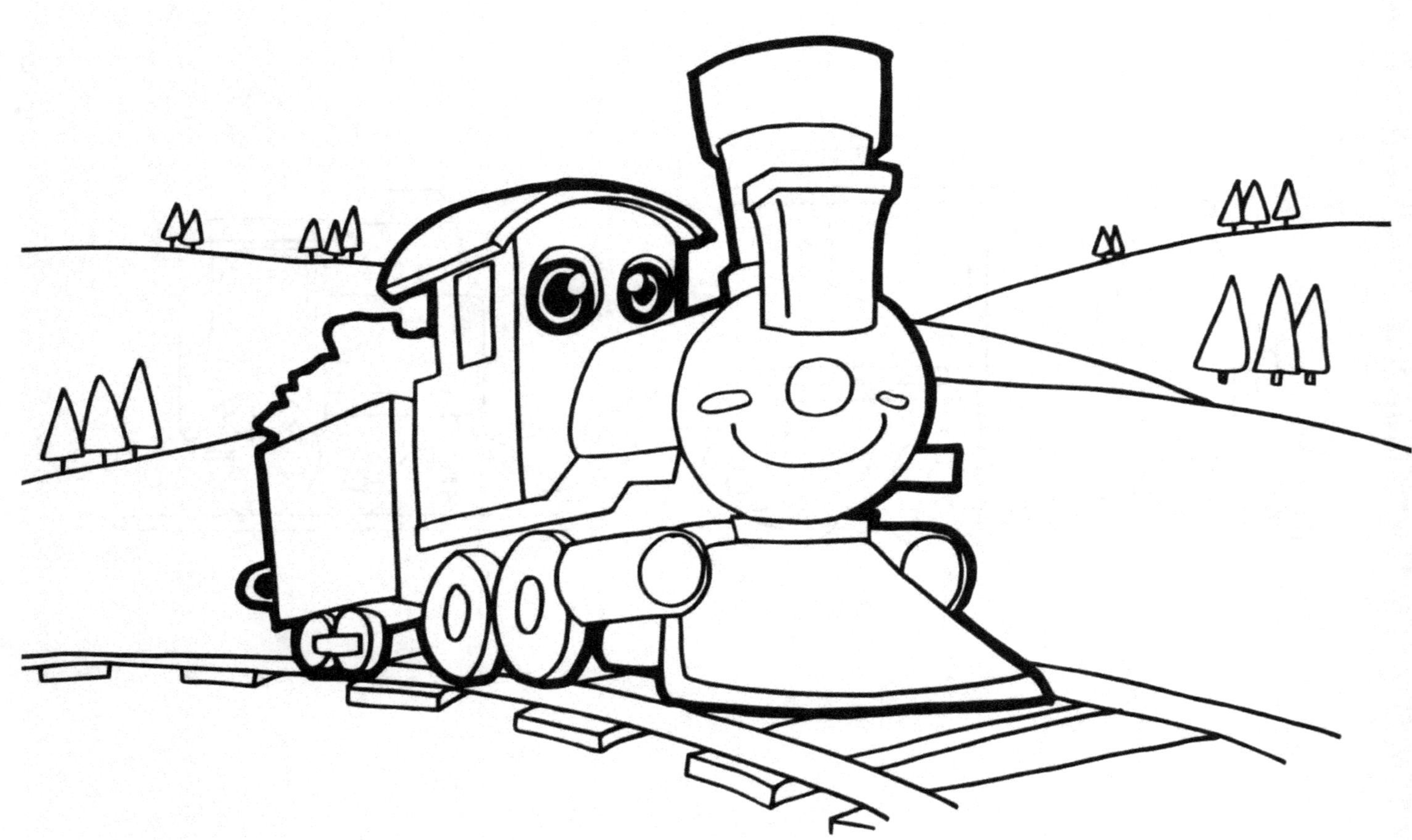

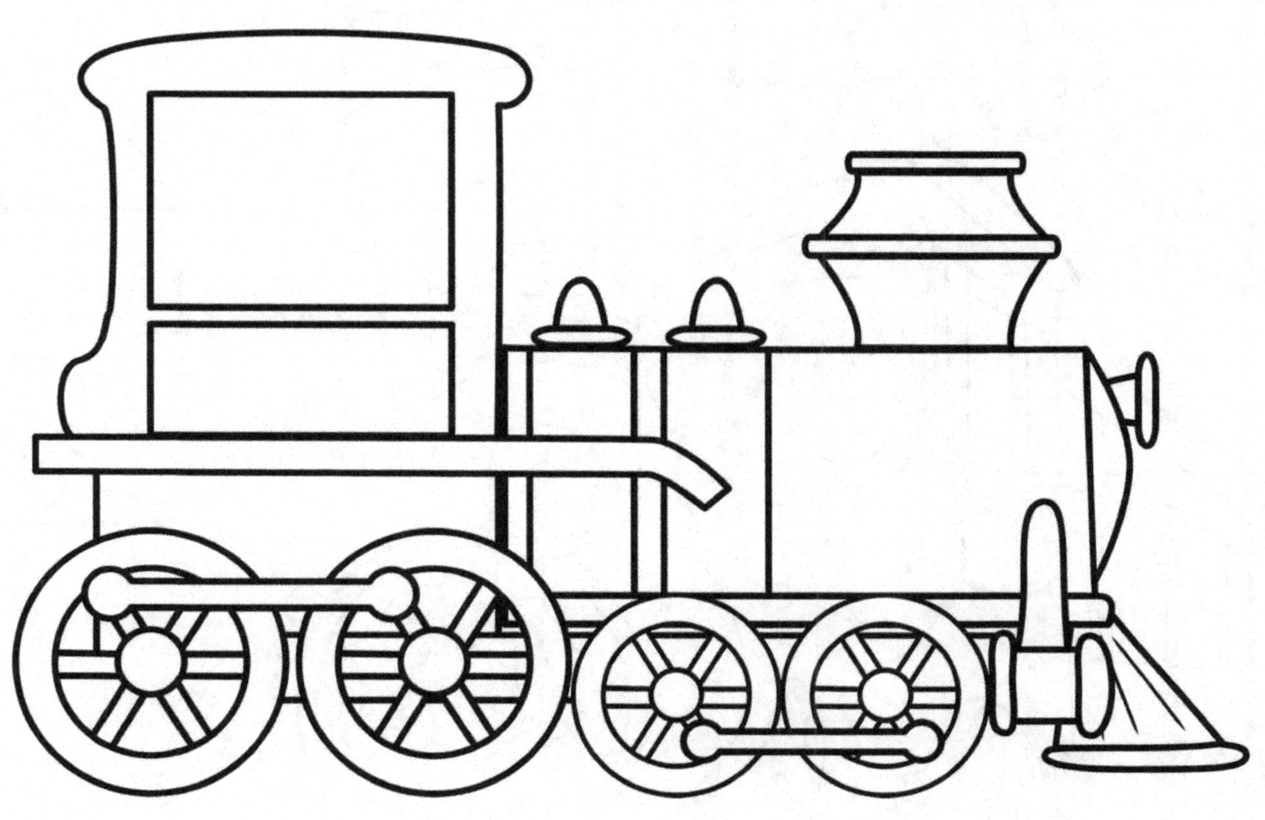

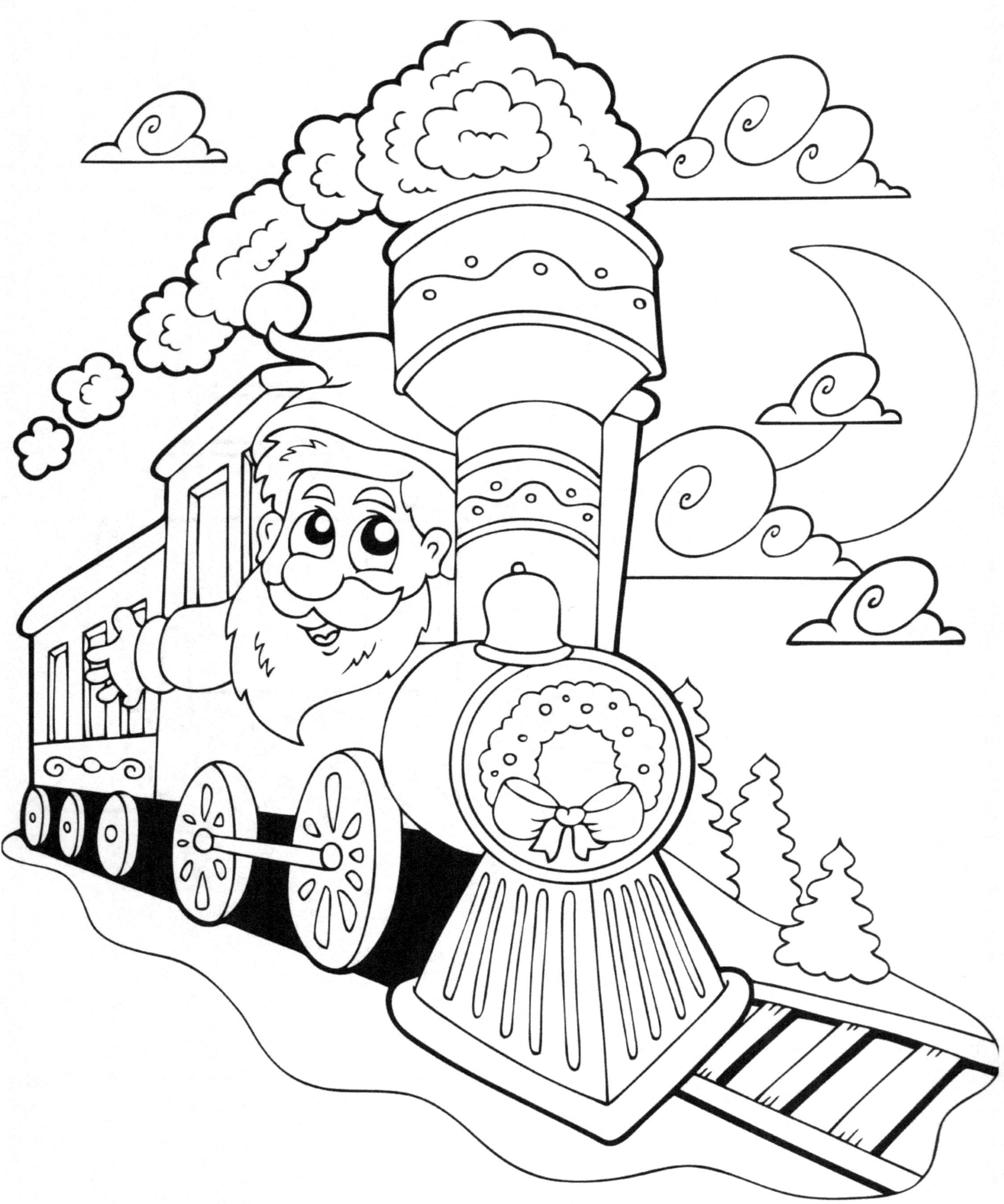

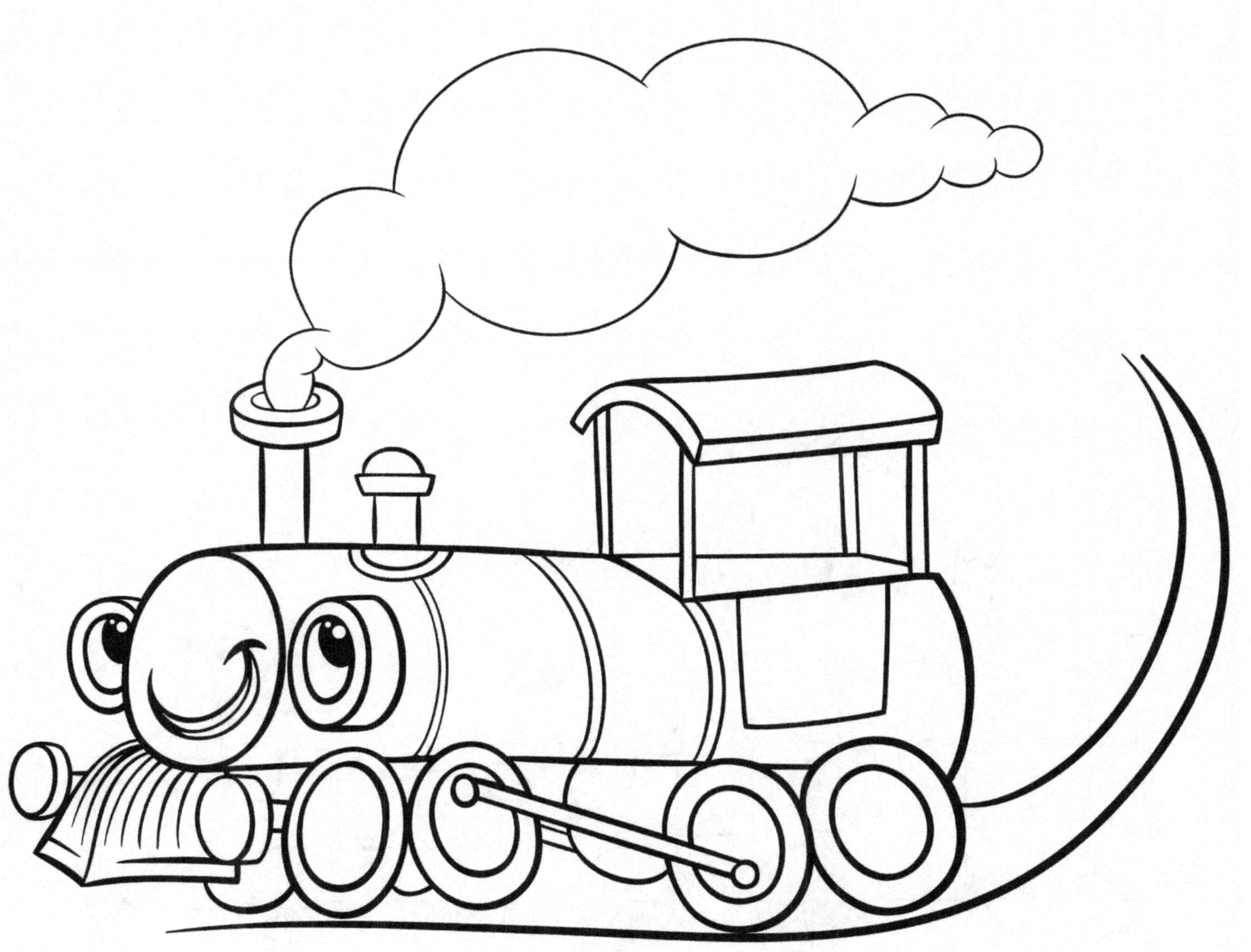

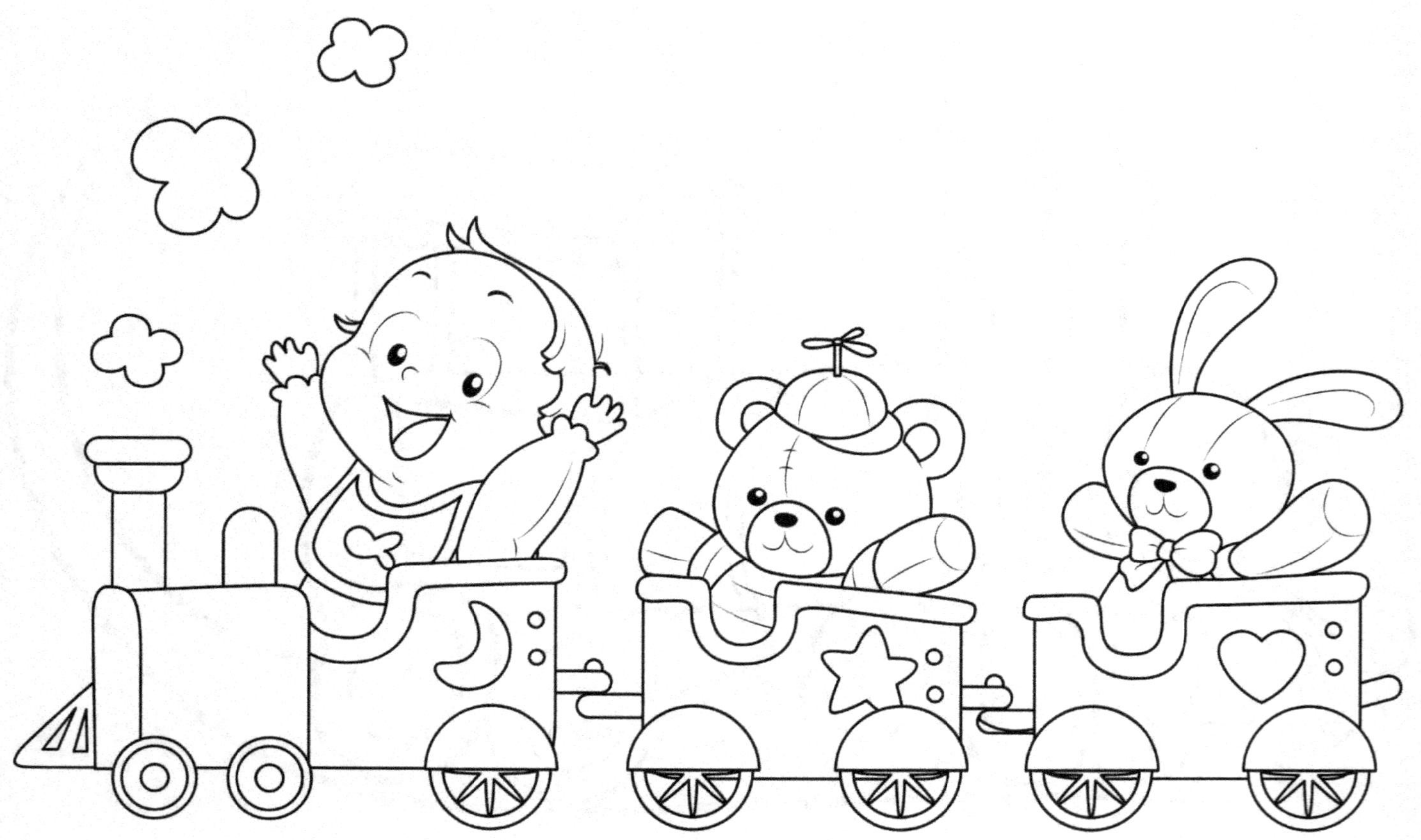

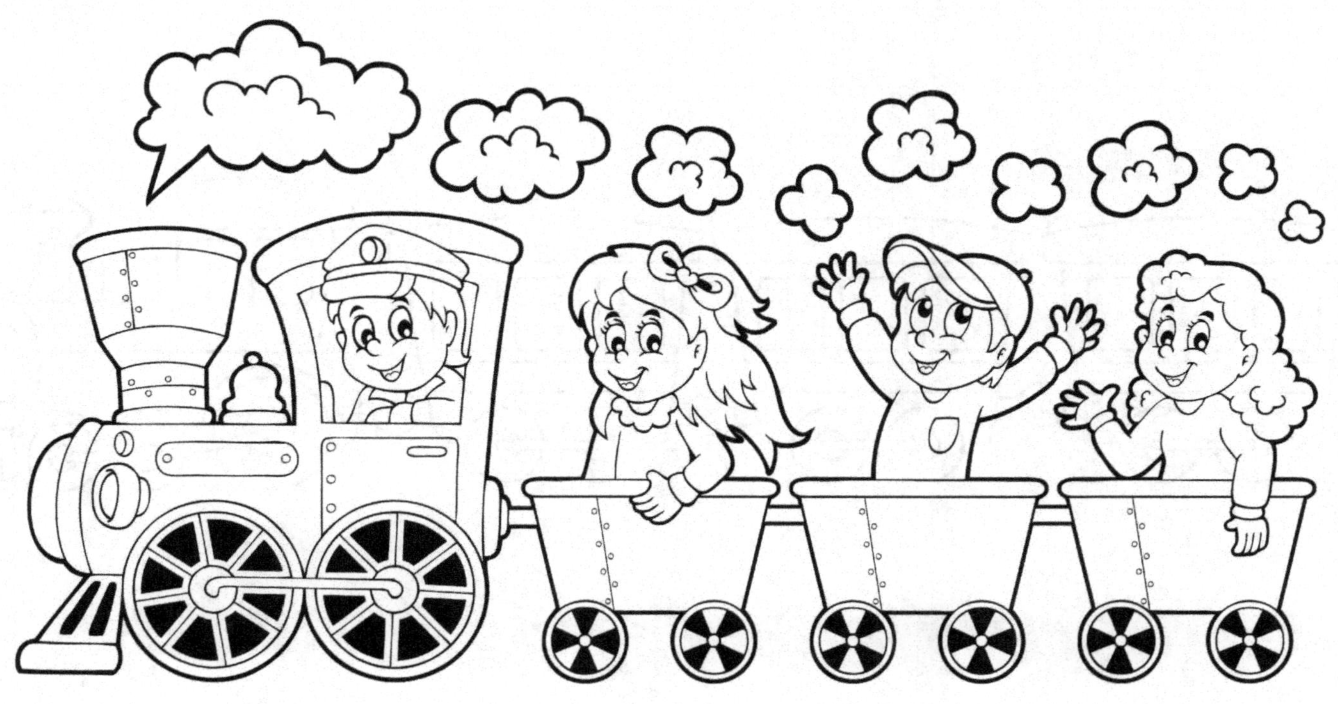

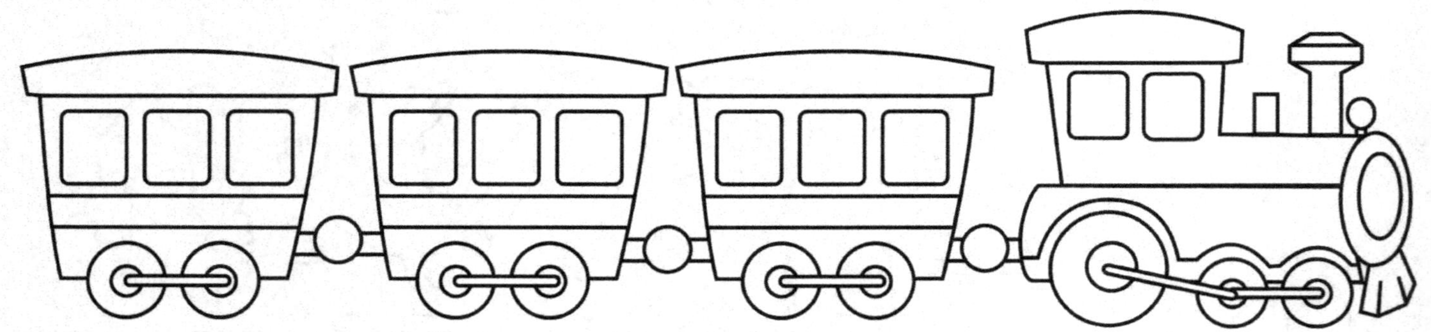

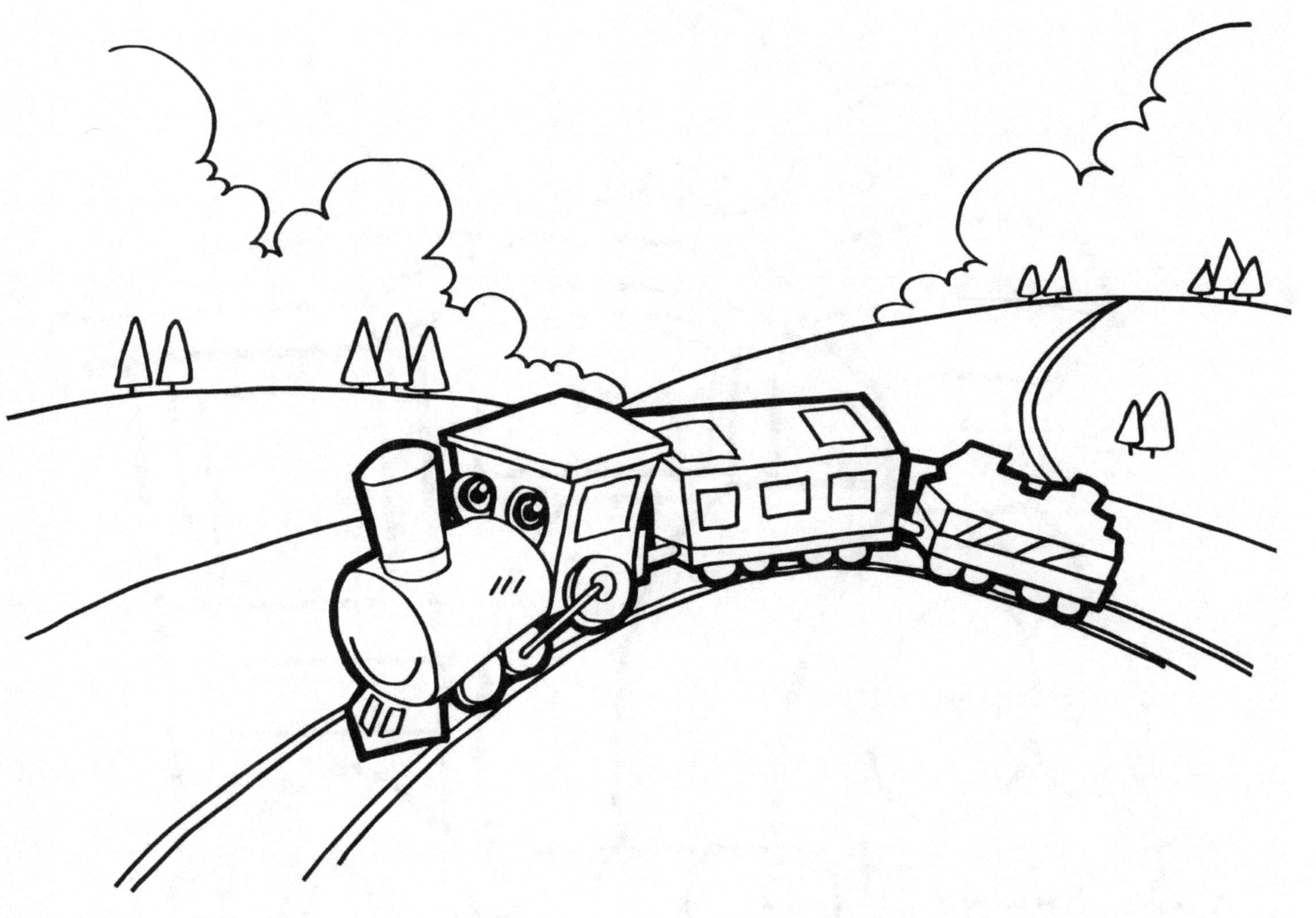

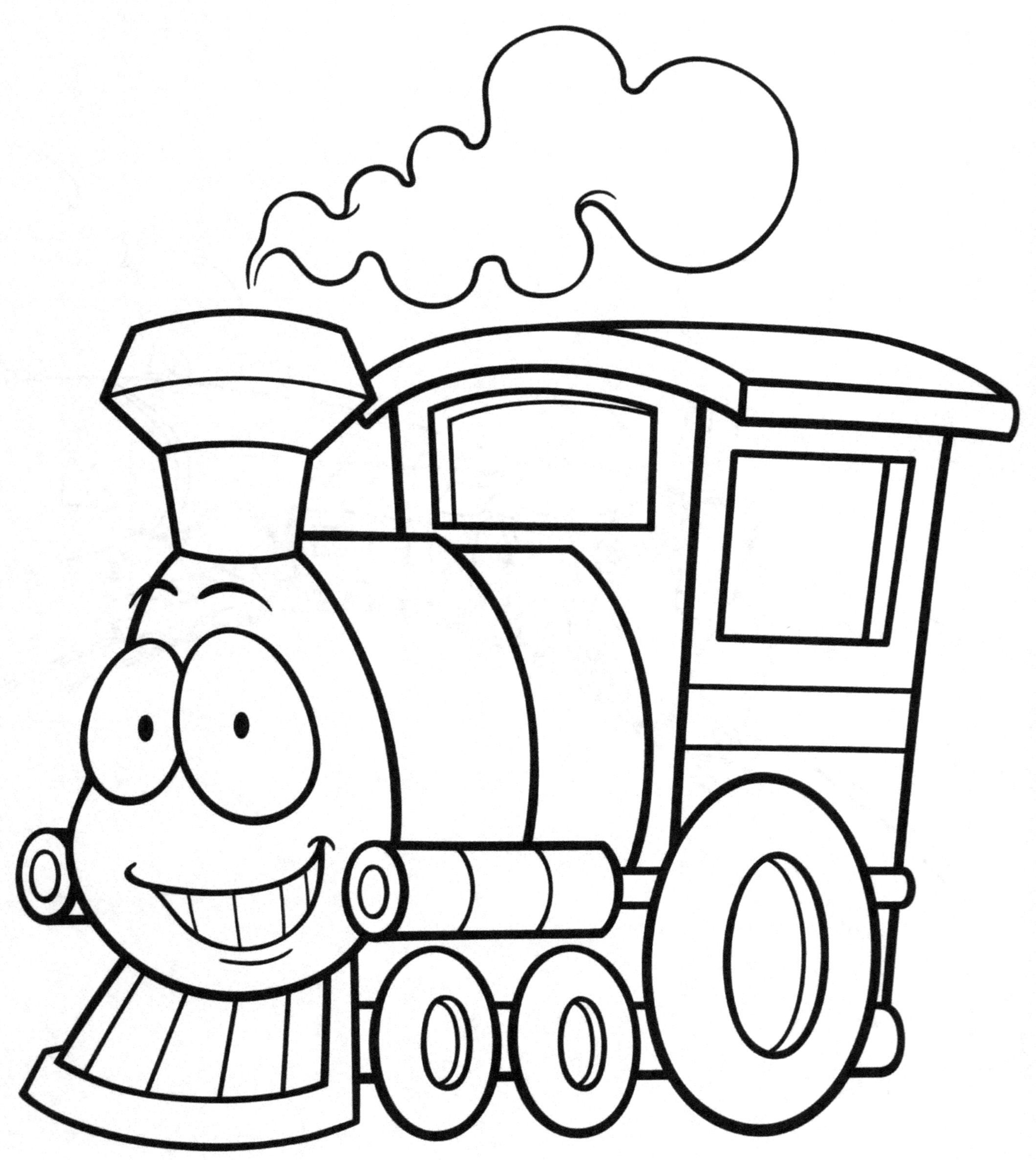

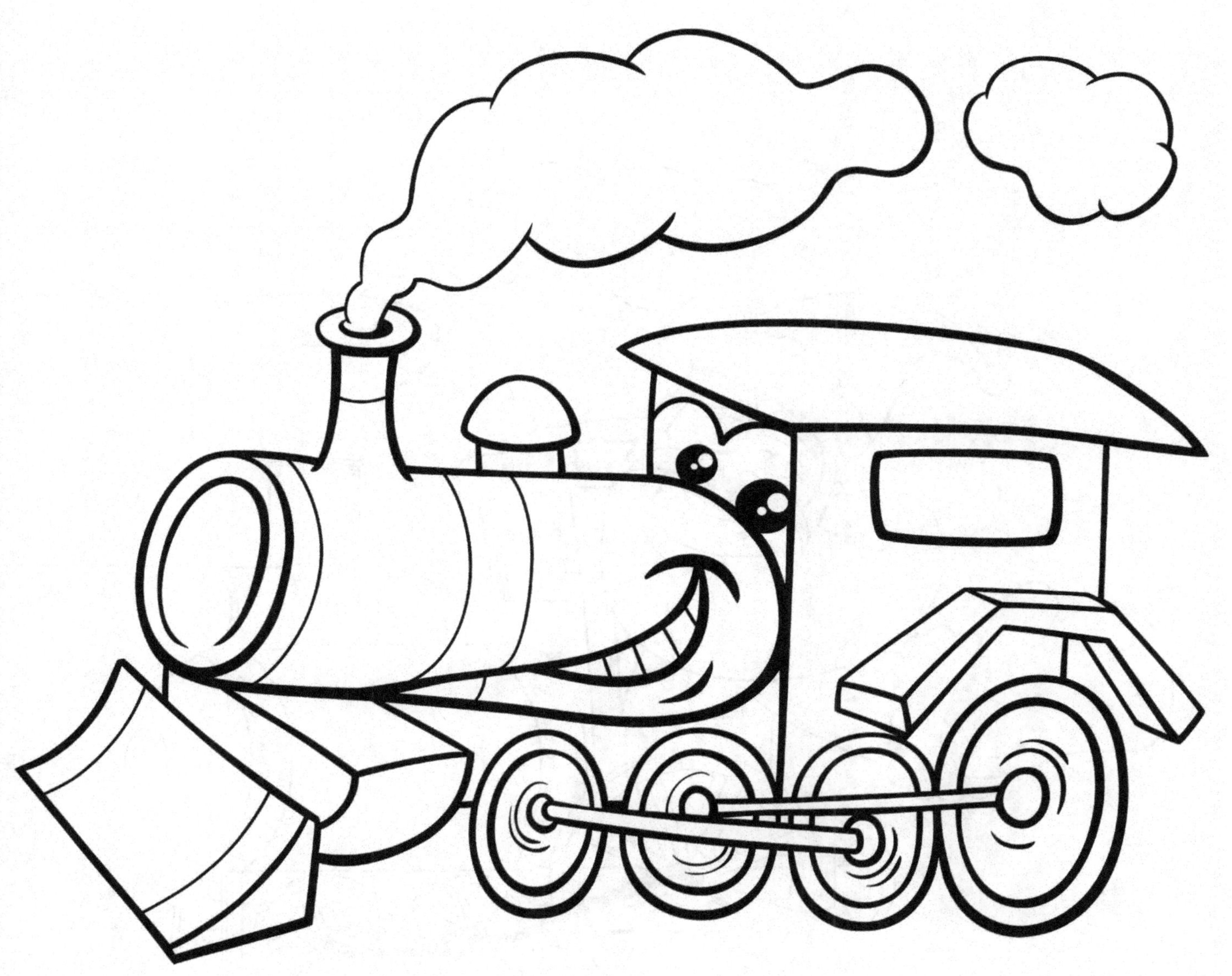

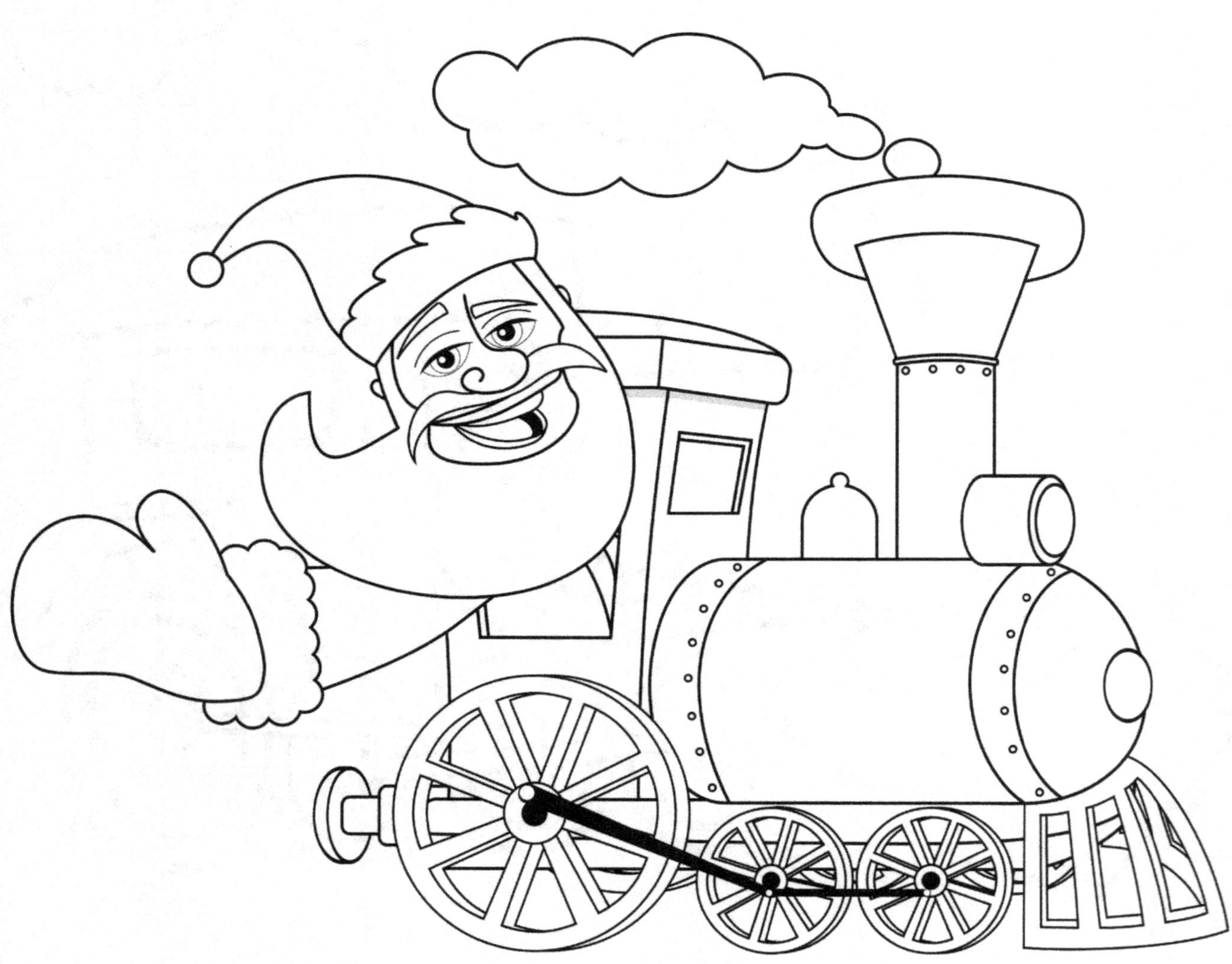

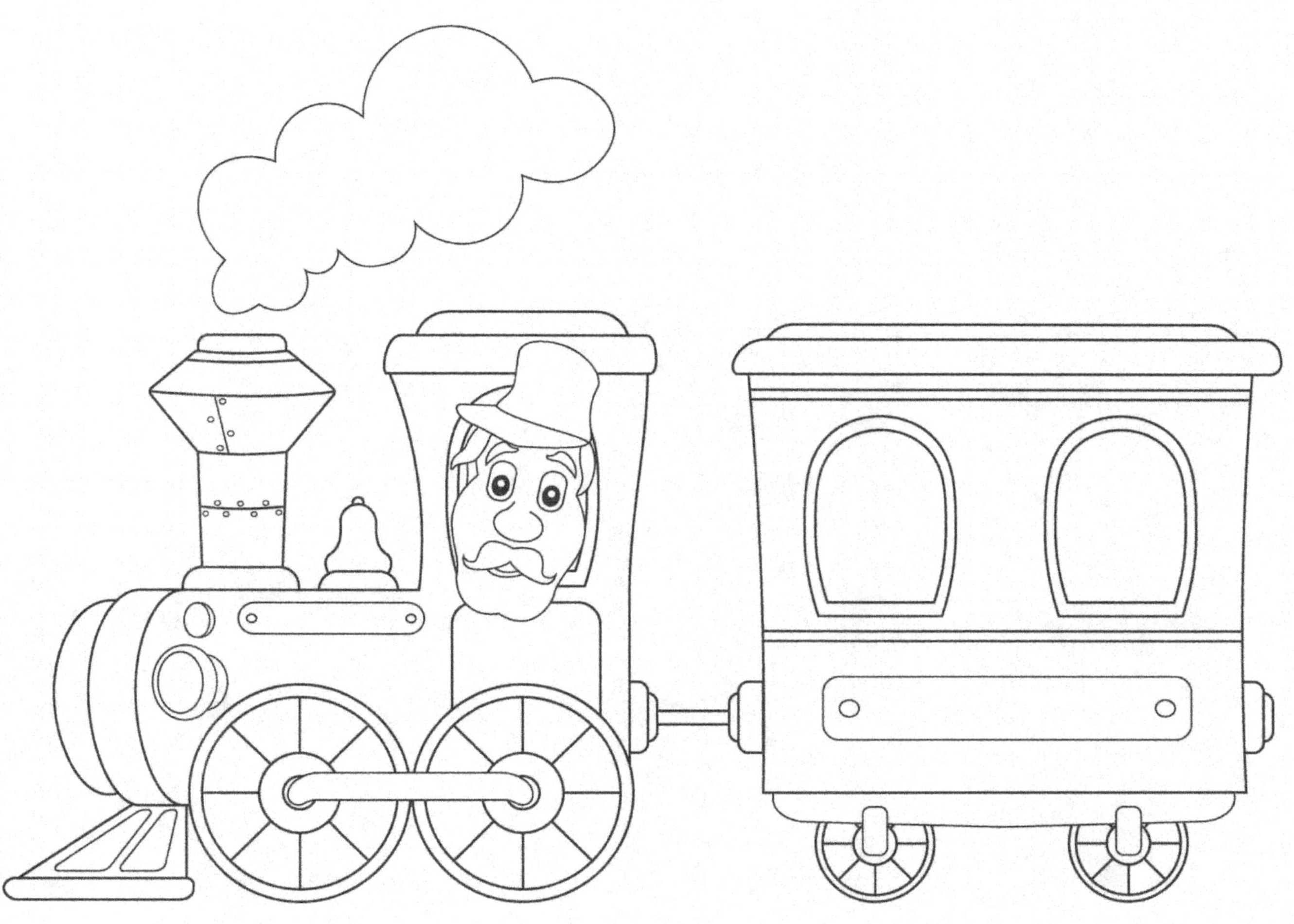

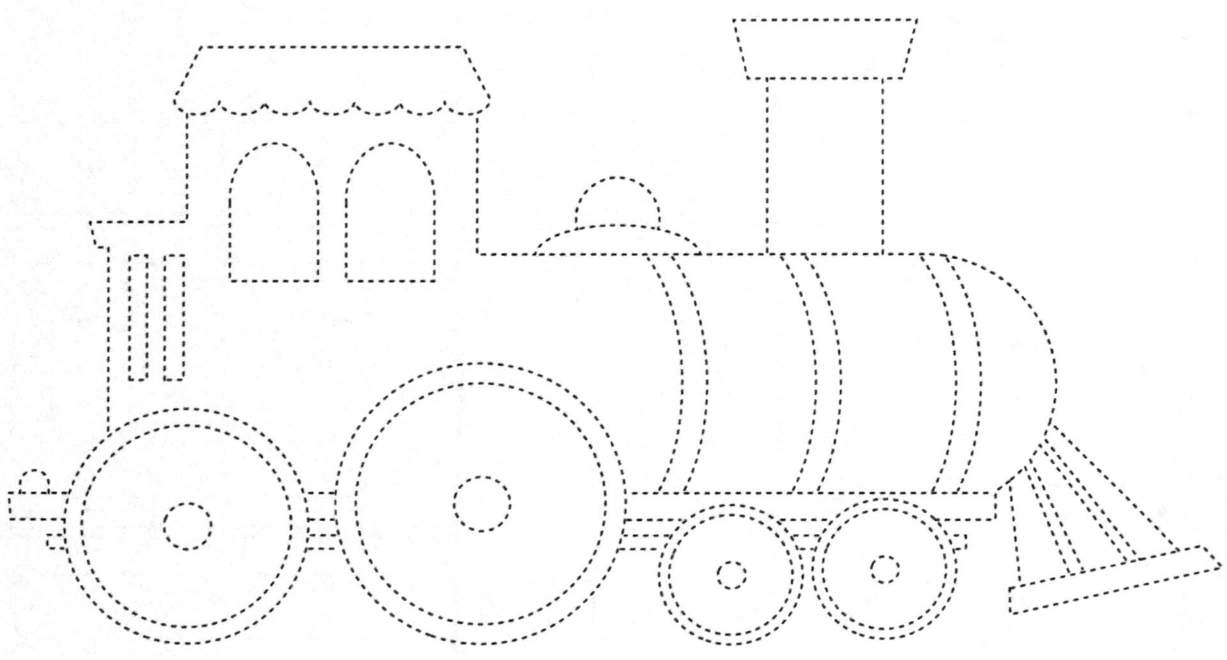

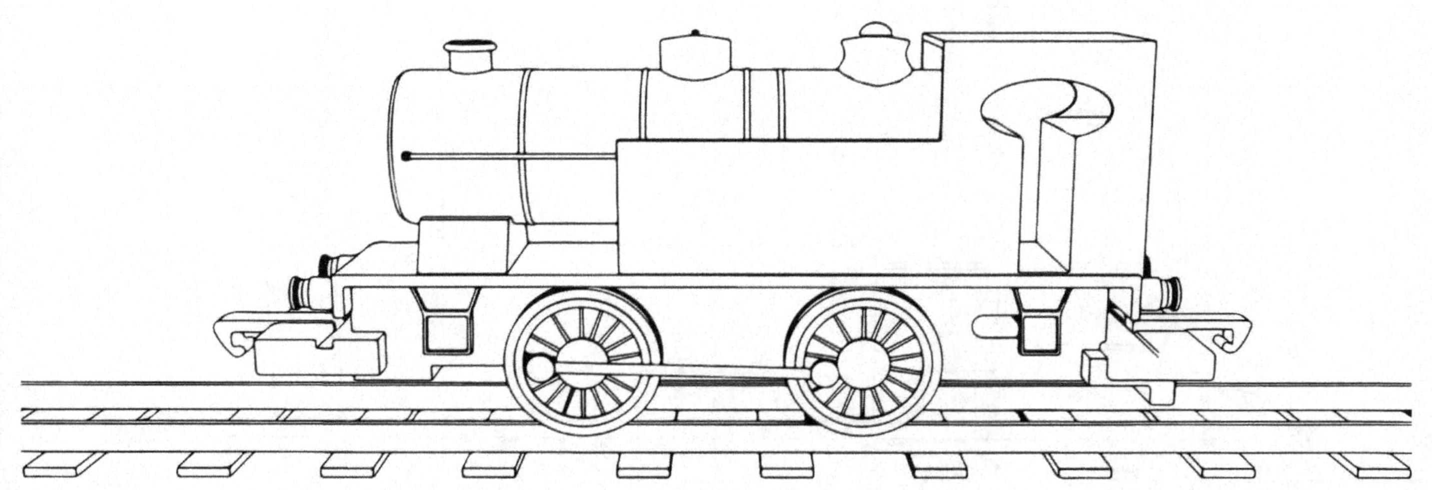

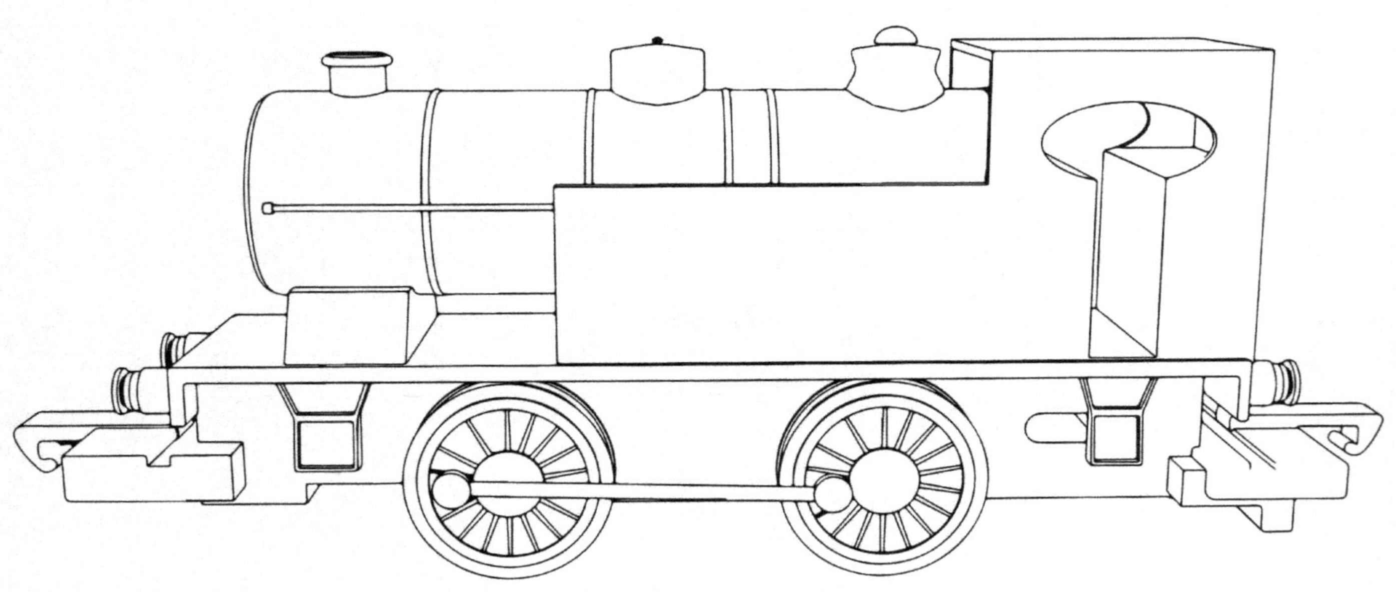

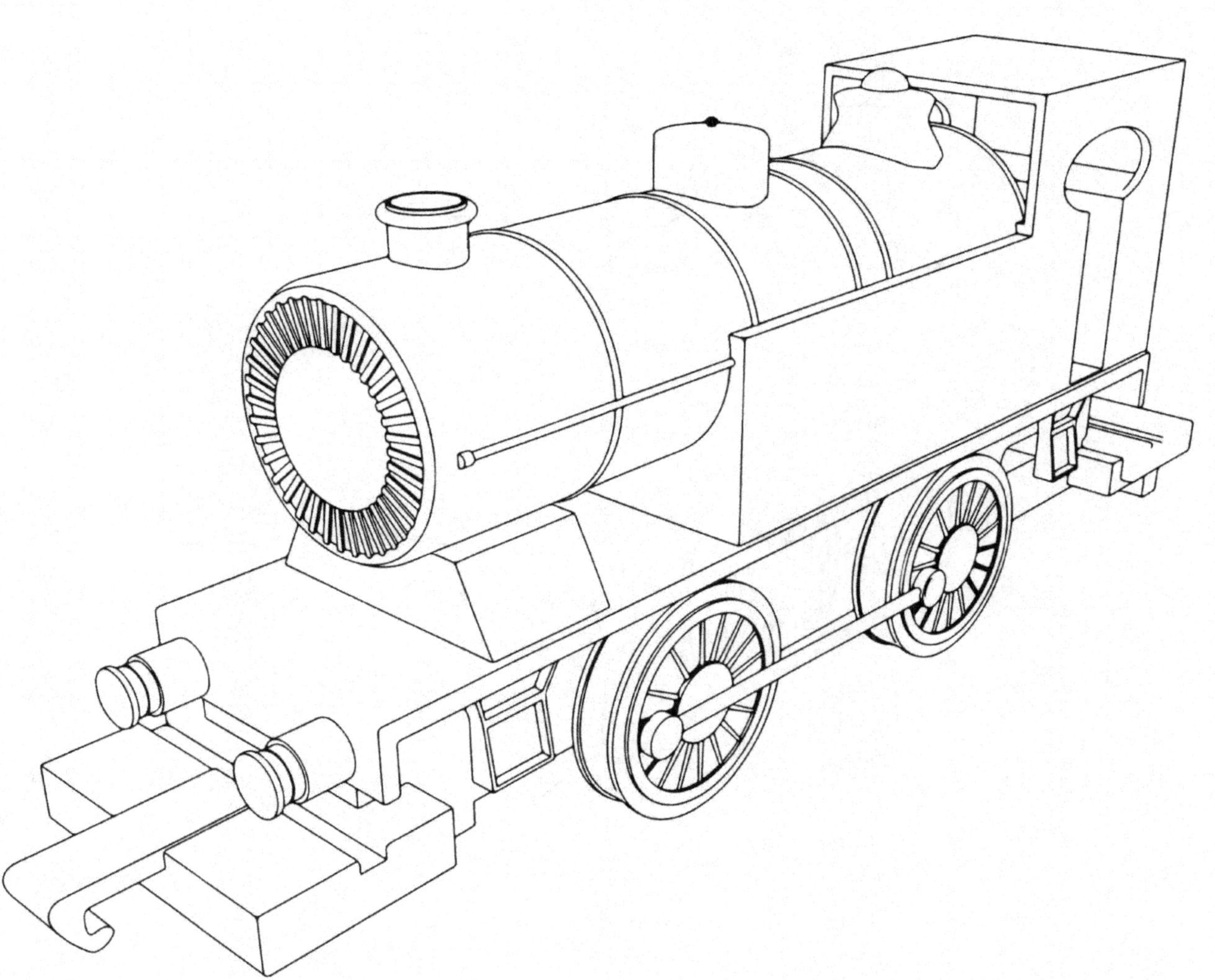

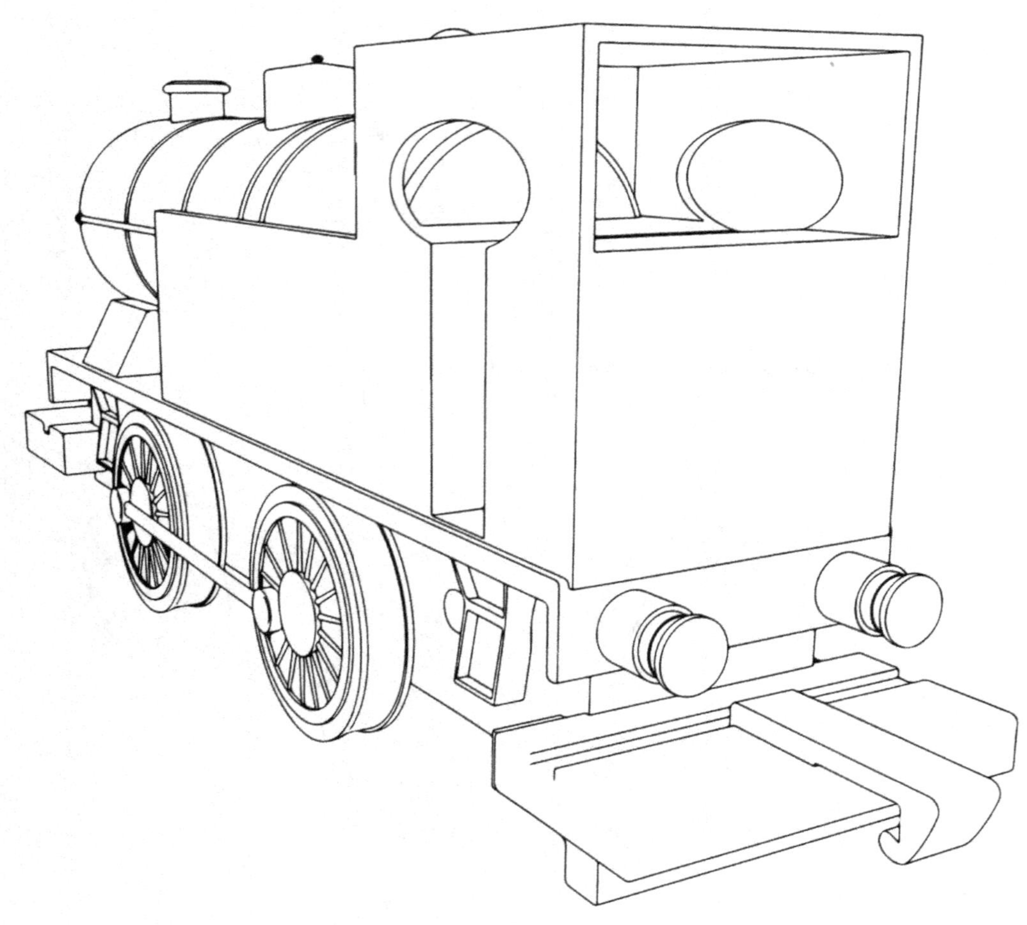

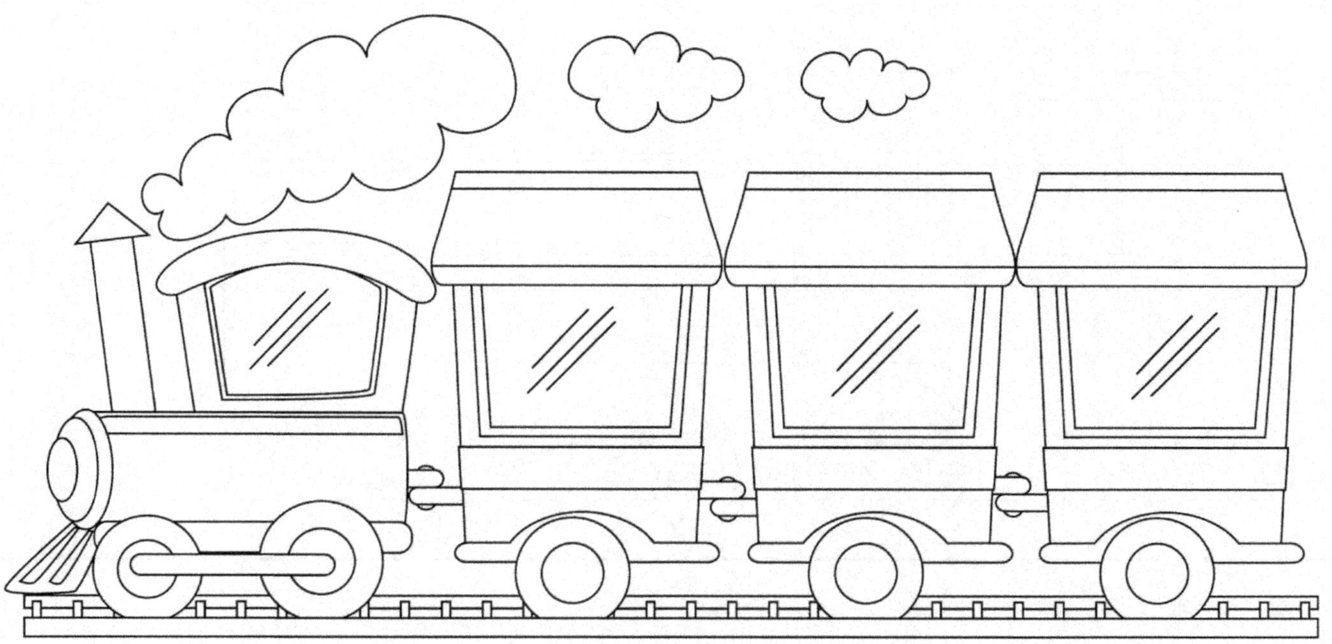

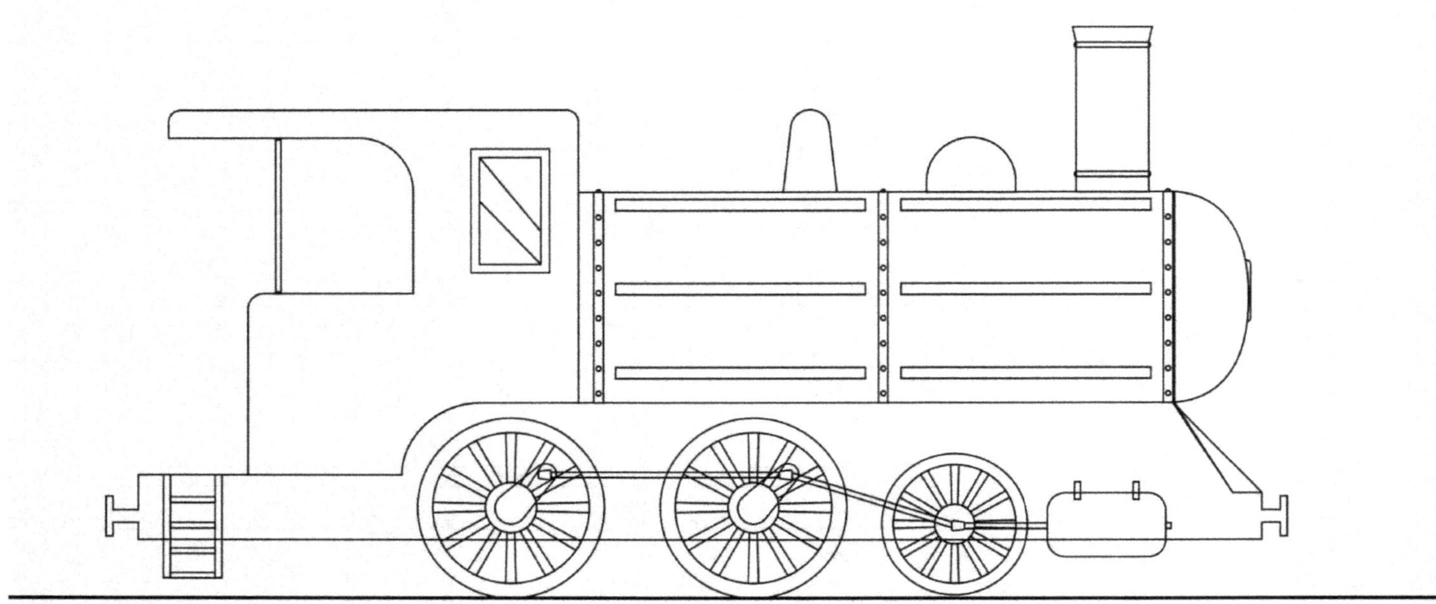

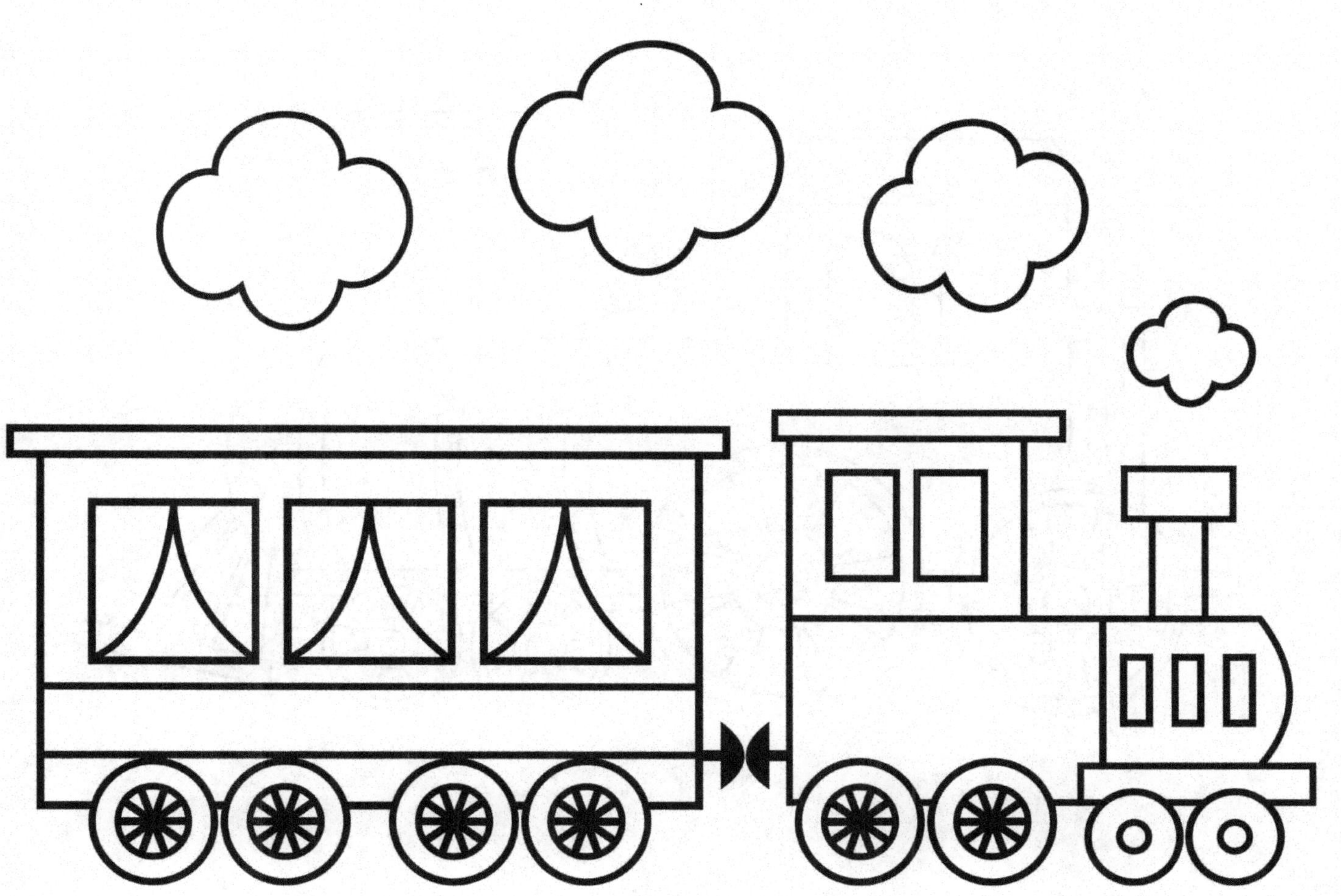

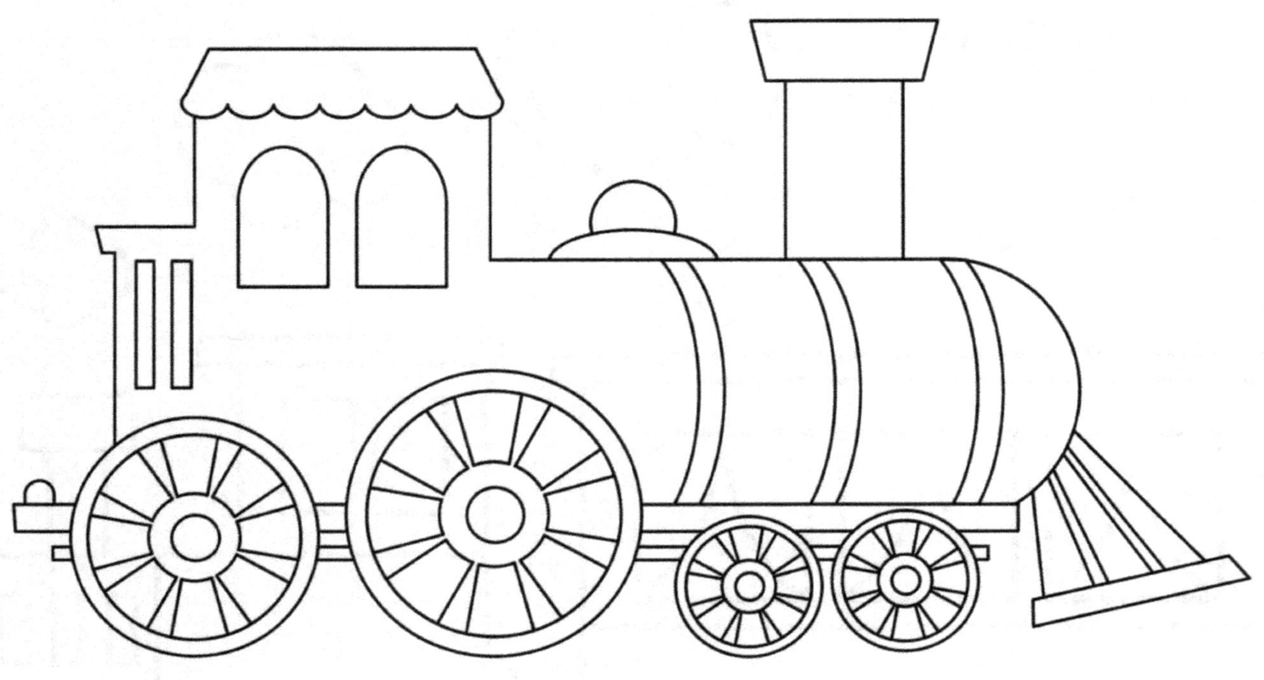

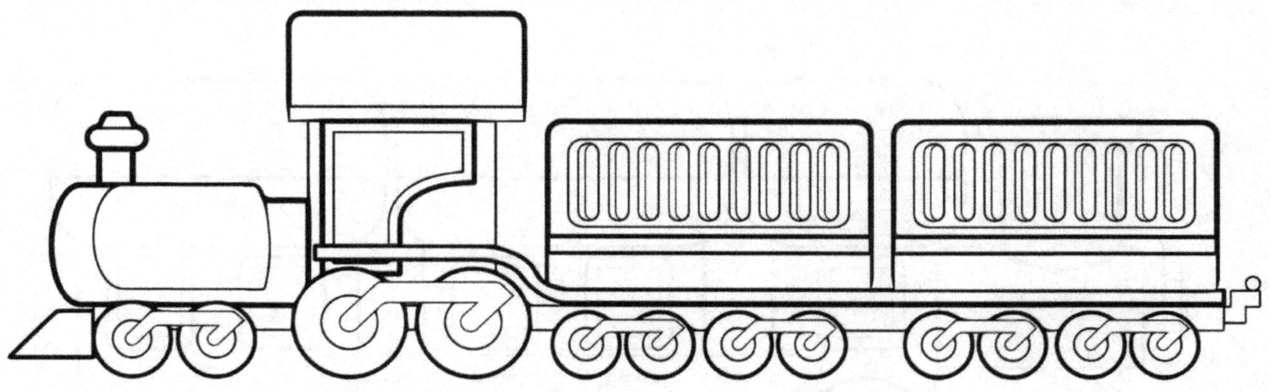

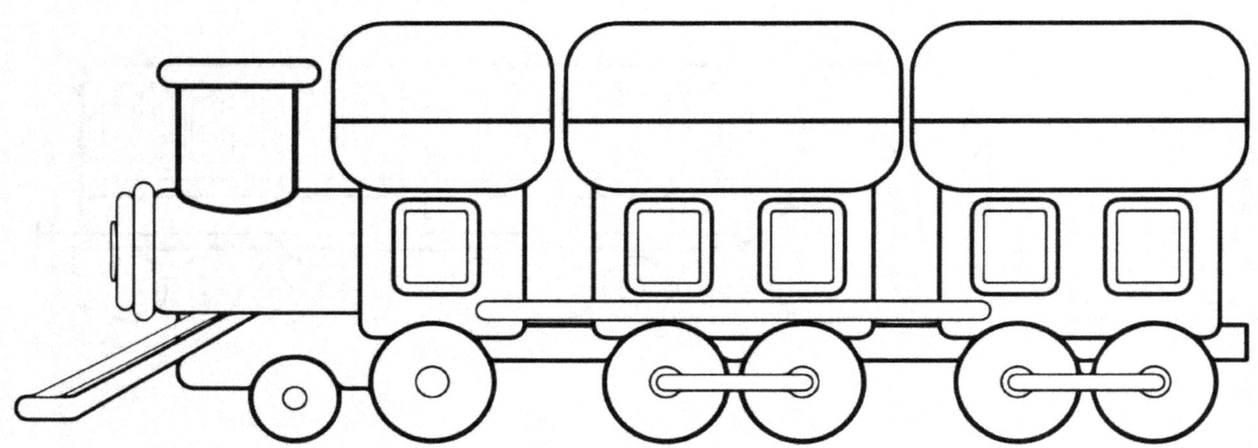